PET OWNER'S GUIDE TO THE
AIREDALE TERRIER

Janet Huxley

RINGPRESS

ABOUT THE AUTHOR

Janet Huxley's love of dogs began as a child, with an Airedale being her ideal choice of breed. It was not until 1984 that she and her husband Tom bought their first Airedale. In 1987 they bred their first litter and registered their Robroyd kennel name. In 1988 they made up their first Champion, Shadli Magnum of Robroyd, and have since had six English Champions, plus another three dogs very near to making the Champion status: Diamond (1 CC & 2 Res. CCs), Black Diamond (2 CCs & 3 Res. CCs), Flint (1 CC-BOB & 3 Res. CCs).

In 1992 Ch Robroyd Emerald was top winning bitch in the breed, and the top brood bitch was Robroyd Crystal. Ch. Robroyd Granite, the only Airedale ever to win 3 CCs in puppy class. He was top puppy and runner-up top dog in 1993, top sire in 1995 and top stud in 1997.

Janet is a Championship Show judge of the breed.

Photography: Steph Holbrook.
Additional photographs: Steve Halifax.

Published by Ringpress Books,
Vincent Lane, Dorking, Surrey,
RH4 3YX, England.

First published 1998
© Interpet Publishing and Janet Huxley. All rights reserved

ISBN 1 86054 009 0

Printed in Hong Kong through Printworks Int. Ltd.

CONTENTS

1

CHOOSING AN AIREDALE TERRIER   7

Selecting a breeder; Registration; Pedigree; Affix; Assessing a litter; Making your choice; The show puppy.

2

CARING FOR YOUR PUPPY   14

Sleeping area; Beds and bedding; Bowls; Toys; Collar and lead; Permanent identification; In the garden; Settling in; Feeding; Treats; Introduction to the vet; Worming; Grooming; Teeth.

3

BASIC TRAINING   26

Socialising; House training; Lead training; Exercise; Sit; Down; The Recall; Barking on command; Dominance; Aggression.

4

THE ADULT DOG   40

Weight; Touch; Keeping fit; Teeth and gums; Nails; Eyes; Ears; Grooming parlours; Shearing; The veteran.

IN THE SHOW RING 47

The breed standard (General appearance; Characteristics; Head; Body; Gait; Coat; Size); Presentation; Step by step guide; Show training; Exhibiting.

BREEDING AIREDALES 62

The stud dog; The pregnant bitch; Whelping; Post whelping; Two to eight weeks; Socialising puppies.

HEALTH MATTERS 72

Internal parasites; External parasites; Parvovirus; Infectious bronchitis; Itchy skin; Anal glands; Heatstroke; Chocolate allergy; Hip dysplasia; Congenital eye problems; Pets beat stress.

1 Choosing An Airedale Terrier

The Airedale Terrier, being the largest dog in the Terrier group is, without doubt, the King of Terriers. He is an intelligent animal, full of charm and character, with the ability to master all kinds of tasks. A little background knowledge of the breed, and its points, adds a hundredfold to the pleasure of owning one of these unique dogs.

He is sometimes said to be 'Jack of all trades, master of none', and perhaps this is because he tries to please so very much that he may want to end a task quickly in order to receive the cuddle and praise he knows are his due, but, given a good trainer, there is nothing he cannot achieve.

The breed originated in the Aire valley in Yorkshire, and it is thought that a variety of breeds or breed types were used in its make-up. In the 19th century, large terriers were used to hunt badger, fox, weasel, otter, water rat and other small game. These dogs excelled in agility, eyesight and hearing, and they also had untiring courage. However they lacked the keen nose and swimming ability of the rough-coated Otter Hound. The two breeds were crossed – and the result was the Airedale Terrier. Bred for courage and tenacity, the Airedale has the true terrier spirit,

A friendly, confident dog, the Airedale is an ideal family companion.

combining the gentleness of a lamb with the courage of a lion. He is confident, impish to a degree, a joker at times, (an Airedale owner must have a good sense of humour) and he can smile – and I do mean smile – when greeted. Active in the garden, or when out for a walk, some Airedales will bunny-hop in circles when excited by play. Throw a ball for him and he will retrieve it many times – but maybe on different days!

Although bred for sport originally, his courageous disposition has been put to use in other spheres. The Airedale has been widely used as a police dog, particularly in Germany, and he has also been used as a despatch bearer in war.

The Airedale will follow his owner anywhere, and in the family environment this gentle giant is ideal as a pet in both suburban and country life. When brought up with children from puppyhood, an Airedale develops great patience, but will move away when tired of boisterous play. He can be a confident guard dog who stands alert if confronted with any situation that he feels requires his deep and loud bark. He will wag his tail and greet another dog in a friendly manner, but if a strange dog shows aggression he will stand his ground and be 'in and at it' with lightning speed.

The Airedale is generally regarded as a strong dog with no serious health problems, and as a housepet he is ideal, because dog odour is practically non-existent in the breed. If a member of the family is allergic to animal hair, many doctors recommend the Airedale Terrier for a pet as he does not shed hair, but does require weekly grooming.

SELECTING A BREEDER
In your search for a new and faithful companion, your first priority should be to find a reputable breeder. A good way to begin is to visit dog shows where you can talk to the exhibitors, watch them preparing their dogs, and see the judging taking place. Some Airedales are sturdy, while others are refined and elegant, so try to find a kennel that is producing dogs of the type that particularly appeals to you. Chat to as many people as you can after the judging has taken place, both at the ringside, and at the benches. Breeders and owners are usually only too happy to answer your questions and help you in your

search for a puppy. The exhibitors are trying to maintain the Airedale Breed Standard, and they put every effort into producing sound, healthy puppies, and giving each one the best possible start in life. In every litter they breed they hope to find what could be the next all-time greatest Airedale!

You can also contact your national Kennel Club for help in finding Airedale breeders. In many cases, a register is kept with details of breeders who may have puppies for sale. You may have to travel some distance as Airedales tend not to be widely bred. Monthly dog magazines and weekly papers also advertise puppies for sale. Airedale Breed Clubs hold up-to-date puppy registers and love to hear from new, and old, Airedale aficionados. Your national Kennel Club can put you in touch with secretaries of clubs in your area.

Seek expert advice when looking for a reputable breeder.

REGISTRATION

Before buying a pedigree dog, always ensure that he is registered with your national Kennel Club. The breeder will give you a signed registration document which shows the parentage, together with details of the puppy's registered name chosen by the breeder, the personal registration number, the date on which he was registered, the breed, sex, date of birth, and colour. If either, or both, the breeder and stud dog owner have had their dogs' hips X-rayed by their vet, both the sire's and the dam's hip-score will be shown on the registration document. Caring breeders hip-score any dog to be used for breeding, as they want to ensure the best of health for their particular breed. The X-ray plate is sent away for scoring by the Kennel Club/British Veterinary Association, or your national equivalent.

PEDIGREE

The pedigree of your puppy, which shows the ancestry of your dog, will also be given to you by the breeder. Each breeder has his own format for the layout of this document. Usually it is a four, or five, generation pedigree, which is signed and dated by the breeder, confirming the details are true to the best of his or her knowledge. For a small fee the Kennel Club can supply a computer-generated certified pedigree.

AFFIX

This is a name chosen by breeders to denote their own breeding lines, and prefixes the dog's registered name. A breeder applies to the Kennel Club to register his chosen affix, for which an initial fee is charged, and thereafter a small annual fee must be paid for its upkeep.

ASSESSING A LITTER

Some positive thinking is required to ensure that the puppy you choose will be the right one for you. He will be with you for all of his life and you will want to share many happy years together. Hopefully, the knowledge you have gleaned from this book and by talking to reputable breeders will have been digested and have given you an insight into the long-term commitment required by you to this particular breed.

Always make an appointment to visit the breeder, as they too have busy schedules, and will want to be able to spend enough time with you. If the breeder of your choice has a strong demand for puppies you may have to reserve one in advance. It is just a matter of waiting for a puppy from a particular bloodline, or looking at other litters. Remember, the decision about which puppy to buy is yours.

The puppies should be of good weight, happy, and in a clean environment, as this usually determines that they will make healthy and happy pets. They should be well socialised, have a good disposition, and love to be around people. Obviously you will see the dam of the litter, and she will give you some indication of how the puppies will turn out.

Temperament is the most important consideration. The bitch should be welcoming and friendly; she should be happy to show off her puppies. Beware of the bitch that appears nervous or over-protective in this situation. In terms of appearance, the bitch will give you some idea of how the puppies will develop, but it is helpful if you can also see other adult dogs of similar breeding so you can get an idea of overall type. It is unlikely that you will see the puppies' father, as in the majority of cases, he will be owned by another breeder. However, you may be able to see a photo of him. If you feel that the puppies are not what you expected, do not buy in haste, but visit other breeders until you feel satisfied with the care of the puppies and their dam.

When you look at the litter it can be bewildering as there are so many points that you are trying to consider. Keep a cool head and

assess the puppies on their merits. Soundness of temperament is crucial whether you are looking for a show prospect or for a companion. The breeder should be able to give you some guidance, and most breeders will also ask you a lot of questions as they are anxious to ensure that their puppies are going to good homes. With a big dog like an Airedale (which grows to approximately 23 inches in height), the new owners must know what they are taking on. This is a breed that makes a wonderful family dog, but it has a strong personality, and firm, fair and consistent training is necessary from an early age.

You will probably have already

Take time to assess the litter before making your choice.

made up your mind whether you want a male or a female. The adult male is slightly bigger, and may need firmer handling than the female, particularly during adolescence. With the female, you will need to cope with her seasonal cycle, although neutering is an option if you have no plans to breed from your Airedale. This operation is generally carried out at a mid-point between the first and second season. Ask your vet for advice.

MAKING YOUR CHOICE

The puppies may be running around on your first visit, or they may be sleeping after a meal. It is a lovely sight to see when you enter the room for the first time.

Many breeders will not let you handle the puppies for fear of infections that you may inadvertently bring in from other dogs you may have, or the dirt on your shoes, for instance. All your clothing should be clean, and a thoughtful person will be extra-clean when visiting the puppies. When visiting, or holding, a baby who has been born in hospital you have to wear a gown, and a puppy is not so different from a human baby.

As you watch the litter of puppies, make a mental note of which are the energetic 'get up and go' pups, and which are the quiet and laid back ones. Do not be taken in by this at first glance. The one who is sitting alone in the corner may seem quiet, but he may be watching his siblings and asking himself "which one shall I choose to play with next?" Many

All puppies have their own personalities, and this should be nurtured and developed during their formative months.

are the times we have sold a quiet puppy who has turned out to be the little darling of the bunch.

Two pups may be scrapping and your immediate reaction may be: "Are they the fighters?" Sometimes they are simply the two that will not back down from each other, both wanting to be top dog. This is not necessarily a problem as, when separated, they could be the two angels of the litter.

In any litter there is always a puppy named Bubbles or Personality Plus and, believe me, there can be more than one. This type of puppy will want lots of attention; he will be clever, and will most certainly wrap you around his little paws

Puppies' personalities are influenced by the guidance, care and sensible attitude shown to them in their formative months.

THE SHOW PUPPY

If you are looking for a show prospect, you will need to look at the litter with different eyes. You still want a happy, healthy puppy, but you will also need to assess the finer points of the breed.

Many times people have said to me: "They look like little Rottweilers." This is because they are very nearly all black except for a little tan around the beard, eyebrows, the crease between the ear and head, and the bottom half of the legs. At this age the shade of tan can give you a good idea of how deep or pale it will be when the puppy is older.

When we choose our pup or puppies we want bubbly personalities, and to see them walk around the room with a certain air about them, the head and neck held well, strutting out in a sure and positive manner, with the tail held on top. The pup usually shows the back line he will have at maturity, something of the balance, and a good tail carriage.

Around the age of four to five months, and sometimes later, your puppy will lose the balanced and cobby appearance and will probably go through a gangly stage, all legs, longer back, tail only just carried. The average pup does grow at different rates; rear legs higher than front, or front legs higher than the back. Keep in mind at this time that your ugly Airedale duckling will become a beautiful swan! Only rarely do you come across a pup that is consistent throughout its growth period. This specimen is rare and is a breeder's dream.

2 Caring For Your Puppy

Having a young puppy about the house is a beautiful experience for any owner. The puppy, being so young and vulnerable, requires the same care as a human baby; the basic essentials being warmth, love, attention, the correct diet, socialisation, a caring and consistent approach to training through educational play, safe toys, and a safe playing area.

Before you collect your puppy, there are various preparations you should make.

SLEEPING AREA

Your puppy's sleeping area requires serious consideration before bringing him home, for this will be his special place for a long time, and he will need to feel safe and secure. Try to keep your puppy where he will be in contact with you for most of the day, and in an area that is warm, easily cleaned, and draught-proof. The best places are the kitchen, the utility room, or even a passageway between rooms. You can partition an area with mesh panels which clip together to give him his own allocated area, or use a lobster-pot playpen, which can be ideal in the

A dog crate will prove a wise investment.

very early stages, but puppies tend to grow out of them very quickly. A dog crate is a more suitable investment that will last for many years, and folds up when not in use. Airedales grow so fast that you should consider buying a crate suitable for a fully-grown dog. A blanket should be put down at the back of the crate for your puppy to sleep on, with newspapers at the front. The water and feed bowls should be placed in the pen on the newspaper. The crate door should be left open so that your puppy can go in and out as he chooses, and he will soon learn to use it for the best reasons; to eat in, to sleep, and to play in and around, but it should not be used as a punishment area.

The crate door can be closed for short periods during training, as puppies tend not to soil their bed area. If you place newspapers at the front of the bed area your puppy can relieve himself, even while the pen door is closed at night when you go to bed. These crates are also ideal when your dog or puppy is travelling in the car, as they fit into the back of an estate car or hatchback so well, and keep him safe while travelling.

When you have been for a walk in the country, and your dog is wet and dirty, what better place is there for him to dry off after he has been rubbed down with a towel? He can curl up on his blanket and sleep the whole way home, and you have no dirty car!

BEDS AND BEDDING
The type of bed you provide for your puppy is entirely a matter of personal choice. The size is very important, so consider how big this will need to be for an adult dog, before you spend your money. Rigid plastic beds are easy to clean and can have a blanket for comfort. The fur-fabric type is not raised from the floor so needs to be washed regularly, and when your dog comes in wet after being outside, even if he has been dried with a towel, his bed will still get wet, so do not let him into this type of bed until he is completely dry. The plastic bed also needs to have the bedding changed at regular intervals.

Wicker baskets and bean bags, especially the latter, are better bought when your puppy has grown up, as both can be dangerous if chewed.

There are many types of bedding specially developed for your puppy or adult dog. Good brands have the advantage of staying dry on top while allowing any moisture to be retained underneath. There are many brand names for this specialist pet bedding, such as Vetbed or Dry Bed, and they have the advantage of being very quick-drying. When taken from the washing machine, all they need is a quick shake, then hang them near a warm radiator and they will dry in about ten to fifteen minutes. They are a little more expensive to buy than a wool blanket, but over the years they prove to be an economical choice.

BOWLS
You will need one bowl for water and one for food. Buy strong bowls that should last your puppy's lifetime. Plastic bowls are dangerous for puppies as they like to chew them! A pot bowl is good to hold the water while your puppy is young as they are less likely to tip over. Stainless steel is a very good buy, especially the non-spill type, and they last a lifetime. If you choose a stainless steel bowl, do buy one that will be big enough to hold enough food for your dog when he graduates to adult-sized meals. As a puppy he

can feed from an old dish from the kitchen cupboard in the early stages, progressing to a full-size dish at about the four-month stage.

TOYS
Just like children, puppies need toys to stimulate their minds, and to chew on, and some thought needs to be given to choosing appropriate ones. Visit a good pet store and ask which are considered the best for puppies. There are so many on the market, some of which are expensive, but, in the long term, safety is the ultimate criterion. Buying cheap toys will be of no value to you or your puppy and you will only have to buy more every time you visit town.

The other point to consider is that your puppy may chew and swallow a cheap and unsuitable

Your puppy will enjoy playing with toys.

toy, and, if this happens, your vet will most definitely have to X-ray your puppy, and perhaps have to operate, so do choose toys carefully.

COLLAR AND LEAD

A collar is essential for your puppy. He may need several different sizes as he grows, so remember this when you are buying one. A long and lightweight lead is also better while your puppy is young. The first collar that you buy should be lightweight, and have a special disk attached with your name, or the dog's name, and your telephone number, or home address, inscribed on it.

PERMANENT IDENTIFICATION

Tattooing is a perfectly safe procedure as a means of identification for your pet. Your vet can tattoo the puppy either on the inside flap of one of the ears or on the inside of one of the back legs, as you choose, and the number allocated to you is placed on a national list. I prefer the ear, as it is easier to access than the inside back leg. In some parts of Europe, breeders can tattoo their animals with a number allocated to their kennel, which is a sensible

You may wish to consider some form of permanent ID for your Airedale.

approach to identifying their animals.

A microchip implant is also available from your vet, and it is a simple procedure for him to insert this into the shoulder of the animal. The microchip contains a personalised number which is registered and kept on a database. The number on the chip can be read by a scanner and checked with the database in the case of theft or straying. There has been much controversy about the chip's ability to stay in place. It was found that the chip can sometimes move to different parts of the body and, ten years after its introduction, this is still a concern for many people. The manufacturers claim they have now developed a chip that is less likely to migrate.

Check that your garden is safe before allowing your puppy to explore.

IN THE GARDEN

Walk around the garden and carefully note all jobs that need attention before your puppy comes home, to make this a safe and secure environment for him. The fencing or walls must be checked, for clever Airedale puppies can find the smallest of gaps, or even dig under fencing. We named a dog Digger for this very reason but, may I add, he did eventually grow out of his digging phase. Check the boundary of your garden before your puppy comes home. Plants look lovely in the summer time, and your Airedale puppy will find them fascinating too; puppies learn from touch, and smell, and the excited puppy will probably try to eat everything and anything he can bite into. It is all down to your approach, so remember they are only babies and speak firmly, but with compassion; the word "No" is sufficient.

The gate should be checked most carefully. Are the gaps wide, and could a puppy squeeze through? It is well worth thinking about attaching a self-closing spring to the gate as a simple precaution, just in case a visitor forgets to shut it.

Your puppy will feel bewildered when he first arrives in his new home.

SETTLING IN

The big day arrives when your puppy is old enough to be collected. The breeder will give you some guidelines about your puppy's feeding routine, when he is next due for worming, and a little advice on basic training.

Do not expect your puppy to be totally happy for the first few days, when he will be homesick for his littermates and his mother. The routine he had become accustomed to has been taken from him and he will not realise he is safe with his new and caring owners.

His new home will seem terribly frightening to him, especially at night when everyone has gone to bed, and he may howl and whimper, not knowing what is happening.

If he cannot adjust, try leaving the radio on at low volume, or place a ticking clock near his sleeping area, and when all else fails, take him, with his bed, into your bedroom for the first few days, just until he gets used to his new surroundings.

When he has become accustomed to sleeping in the downstairs room during the day, he will gradually learn to accept sleeping alone at night.

FEEDING

There are many suitable feeds available and your puppy can have a varied diet depending on your lifestyle. You can feed dried complete foods, meat or tripe, as you choose. The breeder will possibly provide a week or two's supply of the food your puppy has been used to eating to help settle him into your home without changing his regular diet. You may like to introduce different foods once he has adjusted to his new surroundings. The new type of food should be introduced gradually, over a period of days, but do remember that, if the food you have been given is good for rearing the breeder's puppies, then it should be good for your puppy. Many reputable breeders have had years of experience in rearing healthy puppies with good bone, so do keep this in mind if you decide to change the food. You can also ask your vet which foods he recommends when you first visit with your puppy.

A bowl of clean water must be available at all times, and should always be kept in the same place.

Your puppy's morning feed, at 7–8am, is important, as his digestive system has rested for some nine or ten hours so he will be ready for a big breakfast to give him energy for the day. Always serve a good-sized portion of his puppy food and leave it down for about an hour so he can eat at leisure. If your puppy scoffs it all in a matter of minutes, give him a little more until you adjust to his intake capability. Feed to his appetite, remembering that he will need larger portions as he grows.

The second feed should be offered at midday–1pm (is the water bowl full?). This feed routine should be the same as above but this is a good time to offer some variations and different flavours to his meals. Foods which can be gradually introduced to his diet include small amounts of pilchards, sardines, cooked eggs, cooked minced meat, grated cheese, Farleys Rusks (a baby food), and any leftovers from your own meals if they are not too strong in flavour, or spicy.

The third feed at 5-6pm (water!) should be the same as before, again with the addition of a new flavour to the food, but only if necessary.

The fourth feed is given (check the water bowl again!) an hour before you go to bed. This helps your puppy settle for the night. Feed the same puppy brand, but,

if you are to add a flavour, serve a light digestive food rather than something heavy. Farleys Rusks crumbled over the food or a little cooked porridge are good to give at this time. Always take your puppy outside to relieve himself after every meal.

Your puppy will require four meals a day until he is four months old, reducing to three meals a day until he is five months, and then two meals a day until he is 18 months old. These figures are guidelines only, as each puppy is an individual and you should adjust his food according to his needs. Always feel your puppy's body, as his coat can make him appear fat when he may be thin. He should have a slight covering of fat along his ribs. Just behind the ribs his back should be of a good width when feeling from both sides.

A puppy's growth is so rapid during the first six months of life that, when feeding your puppy, always give him a good-quality puppy food at every meal. There are many very good brands of foods on the market specially formulated for each different stage of growth. Visit your local store and choose with care, introducing the new food gradually, over a period of time. The Airedale is still forming bone up to, and sometimes beyond, the age of 18 months.

TREATS

There are many treats you can give your puppy and he will really enjoy this special time with you. You may like to give him some carrot, pear or apple, which puppies do enjoy, but sometimes not until they are a little older. It is important that puppies are supervised when eating the above until you feel confident they can chew them properly. For the very young pup, you can offer puppy biscuits or half a Farleys Rusk, and even a sweet biscuit! When you feel that your puppy is old enough you can introduce a tasty bone (one that is not brittle), or a hard dog biscuit. These are very good to help loosen his puppy teeth to make way for the permanent ones. They also help to keep the teeth and gums clean, by removing tartar and exercising the jaw.

INTRODUCTION TO THE VET

Your puppy must visit the vet, if possible, within 48 hours of purchase. He will need to be examined to ensure he is in good health and his weight is correct for his age. When you first visit the surgery for your appointment, check in with the receptionist and then wait in your car until it is time to see the vet. There may be many dogs in the waiting-room, and a small puppy should not be in an area where there could be infections.

The vet will examine your puppy and tell you when he would like to begin the vaccination course. The protection of an initial course of vaccines does not last for life, so annual booster vaccinations and health checks are important. If you fail to do this it may mean that a full course of vaccination has to be administered for full protection. Hypersensitivity reactions can occur with all vaccines occasionally, and it should also be remembered that there are a few animals who may not fully respond to vaccination.

WORMING

Worming your puppy is important, as even well-reared puppies may have roundworms. There is some controversy as to how many times the puppy requires worming up to the age of five or six months, but your vet will advise on a worming procedure and the exact dosage to give your puppy. I must stress that the dose must be given correctly according to the weight of your puppy, as too much wormer can cause considerable harm, and too little is ineffective.

GROOMING

The care of your puppy's coat to keep it free of knots is as important as combing your own hair. Invest in a good terrier brush (pin pad) and two sizes of comb, one with wide teeth and a fine one.

Your puppy has to be taught table etiquette, which can be achieved by placing him gently on the grooming-table at least twice a week in the early months. He will have to become accustomed to standing for quite a long period when at the grooming parlour, if you choose this method of keeping your Airedale well presented. Any table will suffice, as long as it is non-slip and solid. Your puppy needs to feel safe and happy during this training period.

While he is young and uncertain you may require some help, with one person to hold your puppy and the other to brush him. Hair that has not been brushed can knot and ball up, resulting in

Accustom your puppy to being groomed from an early age so that he will learn to enjoy the attention.

pulling and tightening of the skin, which causes distress to your dog. Do groom at least once a week, making sure that each knot is fully combed out.

The feet need to have the hair cut between the pads on a regular basis, as this hair can knot badly, having much the same effect as a stone in your shoe, and the dog may limp with pain. I cannot stress enough the importance of checking this at least every month or so. It is a good idea to accustom your puppy to having his feet washed after going out for a walk. Fill a bowl with water and place it outside, by the back door, in readiness to wash his feet on returning from your walk, so that you have no dirty paws treading into the house.

Tiny hairs grow inside the ear canal and you must pull the hairs out carefully so that the ear canal is clear and air can circulate. The simplest way to deal with this is by pulling just a few hairs every so often, using your forefinger and thumb. Practise this simple task yourself or ask the grooming parlour to do it for you. Watch your puppy for headshaking, as this can be the signal that his ears need attention.

When you have finished grooming, give him a fuss and a treat while he is still on the table, so he associates grooming with a happy event. Always play with him afterwards so that he understands that it is all part of his routine. Never lose your temper during this training or he will never forget and your task will be harder the next time he is placed on a table.

TEETH

Teething can be a difficult stage for some puppies. Always check the teeth to see if any are loose, and use a baby teething gel on his gums if he is suffering a little discomfort .

Your puppy's milk teeth should be checked regularly, and loose ones may need to be removed, with some help from you. The best approach is to give him hard biscuits, or a safe knuckle-bone to chew, and they will soon come out. If the top teeth overlap and the bottom teeth fit snugly under them the dog is said to have a scissor bite, whereas when the top and bottom teeth are equally balanced he has a level bite. Both are normal.

Sometimes the puppy canine teeth protrude slightly into the roof of the mouth but this is not a problem unless your puppy seems to be in pain or has difficulty chewing his food, in which case you should consult your vet. He may snip the point of the tooth until it falls out naturally.

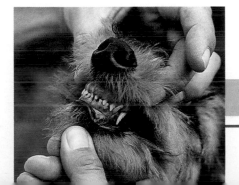

Check your puppy's teeth regularly, particularly when he is teething.

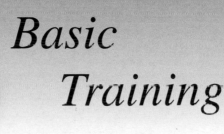

Basic Training

Routine and consistency are the key factors when training, and the same simple procedures should be followed by all the family.

Airedales always want to please, but should not be pushed to the limit, as you will end up with a frightened and nervous dog. Let the puppy grow happily, learning through play, using his favourite toy, a ball, or food to encourage him. Do not repeat a lesson too many times or you may bore him; one session lasting a few minutes, successfully achieved, is enough. He will learn a great deal if you praise him at the appropriate time, and if he has to be chastised, the word "No", spoken in a firm voice, with a growling intonation, is sufficient. Always remember it is useless to reprimand a dog for wrongdoing unless you have caught him in the act. To correct a misdemeanour later will only confuse and distress him as the poor dog will never understand.

SOCIALISING

Socialising your puppy is one of the key elements in owning a well-adjusted dog. Until his inoculations are complete, your puppy cannot go out in an area where other dogs may have been. However, you can still start on the correct path by allowing him to say hello to visitors. Do not shut him away when people call; he is, after all, part of the family and should be allowed to mix and socialise. Ask your visitors, adults and children, to approach your puppy with their hand held low, palm upwards, letting the puppy come to them to be stroked under the chin. Too many times I have seen people lift their hand and swing it down towards the puppy to stroke him on top of the head. Approaching him in this way may make the puppy think he is going to be hurt.

As soon as possible take your puppy out and about to meet

Socialisation is the key to having a calm, sensible dog who will take all situations in his stride.

people. Ask them to stroke him, but do not let them pick him up. Puppies wriggle when held and can easily be injured if dropped. If he growls at strangers and tries to snap, stop him immediately, speak harshly to him and say "No", using the growling intonation again. Afterwards ask yourself what caused the situation, and try to analyse the reason for it. Something may have upset him, but nevertheless, he should not be allowed to show any aggression.

Let him play with other animals, as long as there is not likely to be any danger to him, and he is less likely to become a 'fighter' when he grows up.

Puppies are curious about their surroundings and need to adjust to different noises, traffic and the environment. Take him out in the car with you, even if you are only going to the local shops, which will help him become accustomed to the noise and movement of the car. If he is car-sick, try leaving it for a short while and then begin again with shorter journeys until he has overcome the sickness.

Puppies tire very easily when they are playing, so do not run his little legs off, and make sure he has a good rest at certain times of the day. This will also help him become accustomed to being left alone for short periods.

HOUSE TRAINING

Young puppies need to go outdoors many times in the day to relieve themselves. Begin by taking him out about once every hour, and always after a meal. Praise him when he has relieved himself as this will give him confidence, and then play with him afterwards. You will soon be able to judge how many times he will need to go out in a day.

If you have invested in a crate, you will find this a great aid to house training. No dog likes to soil his own bed, and so if he is in a confined area, it is an incentive to be clean. Obviously, a young puppy cannot be expected to be clean at night, so, to begin with, it is a good idea if you put the bedding in the back of the crate and newspaper at the front. You will find that the puppy will use the newspaper if necessary. In fact,

it is surprising how soon a puppy will learn to be completely clean in his crate.

Each puppy is different; some can be toilet-trained very early and some much later, as it depends on the age they become mentally and physically mature enough to accept this training. Always give praise and kindness when your puppy achieves the correct result, but never rub his nose in the accident!

Reprimanding your puppy with a rolled-up newspaper can make him head-shy, so that he becomes withdrawn, hiding in a corner every time you walk in the room. A puppy will cower from his owner if he is chastised every time he soils the home. It makes me very sad when a puppy reacts like this as he should always greet his owners with a happy outlook.

LEAD TRAINING

This part of training is a pleasure, and humorous to some degree when looking back over the years, but it can be a challenging period for the inexperienced owner.

The best approach is to start as soon as possible, using a very lightweight extra-long lead, or you can make your own about two metres long. By this stage your

Do not put pressure on your puppy when he is learning to walk on the lead.

puppy will be accustomed to wearing his collar, so begin in the garden where it is safe and have tidbits available to attract his attention and give him if required. Attach the lead to his collar and follow your puppy wherever he goes, without letting him become aware you are able to restrict his movement.

Spend a little more time on lead training each day. Talk to him and try to keep him at your side, but, if something takes his attention and he begins to run, keep at his side, or give enough lead so he can charge off in front. Never let the lead jerk on his neck, and if he

struggles and panics, relax the tension, or take the lead off and try another time. Continue in this way until he walks at your side, or a little in front.

Eventually, as his confidence grows, he will want to please you and stay by your side. Sometimes a young Airedale will take to the lead like a duck to water, but do not be upset if this is not the case with your puppy. Take your time and try him every other day, or twice in the week.

EXERCISE

Most owners cannot wait to take their new puppy out for a walk

In time, your Airedale should walk at your side on a loose lead, without pulling ahead or lagging behind.

short free run if you have access to a safe area. This can be built up gradually during the growing period.

Once he is about twelve months old, you can extend his walks from half an hour to an hour. Always monitor your dog when out for his walks, making sure he is fit and well. Walk early morning or late evening during the summer, but never in the hottest part of the day, as dogs suffer from the heat, especially black-coated animals such as Airedales. The same rule applies if they are cooped up in a hot room with the sun shining full on the windows, and, of course, dogs should never be left in the car on hot days, even if it is only for a short period, as they can die from heatstroke.

once the inoculation programme has been completed. However, it is very important not to over-exercise youngsters. The Airedale puppy has a lot of growing to do, and problems can occur if too much strain is put on developing bones and joints. Start off with short outings, giving your puppy the opportunity to get used to the sights and sounds of everyday life. Lead-walking should be confined to ten to fifteen minutes, with a

BASIC EXERCISES

Training should start from the moment your puppy arrives home. This does not mean that you should embark on formal training sessions – this would be a big mistake as puppies cannot concentrate for long periods. However, learning can be developed through play.

You attract your puppy's attention every time you call his name, and when his food is to be

If necessary, the Sit command can be reinforced using gentle pressure on the hindquarters.

work. It is the tone in which you speak that is the key to training. A praising voice, a happy voice greeting him, and occasionally an angry voice, will be used throughout his life.

Toys are also a good way of gaining attention. Hold the toy in one hand and ask him to "Watch". When you have his full attention he will look at you directly, then hold him gently under his chin so that he can see you put the toy down a little way in front of him. Let him look at the toy and then ask him to "Fetch". Change the toy, and the mode of play, occasionally because an alert puppy can easily become bored with repetition. In time he will become accustomed to the actual word you use, and you will be amazed at his ability to build up a vocabulary.

SIT

Meal time is the best opportunity to teach this exercise. You want your puppy to learn to listen to your voice so, when serving his meal, ask him to "Sit", in a light voice and emphasising the 'T'.

If he does not respond, put one hand under his chin and the other hand on his back, gently lifting the chin upwards as you apply gentle

served. This has been taught to him from the beginning by his breeder who would have called to the puppies when she came into the room. You must continue to do this if you are to develop his ability to concentrate. Use his name every time you want him to listen to you.

In the beginning, the actual words do not mean a lot to a young puppy but your voice, used with the correct intonation, will

Down is a useful command to teach and can be a lifesaver in an emergency.

pressure on his rear end, pushing him to the floor. Say "Sit" again, to reinforce the command.

DOWN

This is a useful command to teach, and, if your dog will respond instantly to the "Down" command, it could prove a lifesaver in an emergency situation.

Start by putting your puppy in the Sit position, and, holding a titbit, lower your hand to the ground. In most cases, the puppy will lower himself into the Down to follow the titbit. Once he is in the correct position, give the command "Down", and reward with the titbit. Repeat the exercise, encouraging the puppy to stay in the Down for longer periods. The aim is for your dog to respond to the "Down" command when he is at a distance from you.

THE RECALL

Once he recognises his own name, you can begin to train him to come back to you on command. First let him burn off a little steam, free running in the garden, or a safe area. Airedales do love free running and should always be allowed this pleasure. When you think he has had enough free play, call him by name and shout "Come". He may not do it straight away, but when he does, give him a tidbit. Treat it as a

The Recall exercise should be built up gradually.

Training sessions should be fun, so intersperse teaching with play.

game, and your perseverance and patience will win in the end, even with your delinquent Airedale.

A long washing-line, tied to his collar, is best used for the Recall. Leave the rope loose at your feet and send him out on the field. When he has gone out far enough, but is still able to hear you, call him by name. If he will not obey, stand on the rope and tug it to stop him from venturing further. Call his name again, and bring him in slowly using the rope, and praise him. Send him out again with a command such as "Go on", so he will not feel he is going to miss his free running. Keep changing tactics, through play, to keep him alert and make him feel the time spent with you is enjoyable.

As with humans, your dog will not always be on top form, so when this happens, give him a day off. It is far better to learn a little each month with slow progress, than to rant and roar at him when he has not understood.

BARKING ON COMMAND

When teaching a puppy to "Speak" you have to wait for the correct time to encourage him. When he barks, say the word "Speak", and in time he will be aware that you are asking him to bark. A favourite tidbit is good at this time. Ask him: "Do you want this? Speak." The puppy may not know what is being asked of him at first, but one day the penny will drop and he will bark. When someone rings the door bell, encourage your puppy to bark, and praise him when he has made a noise. Introduce him to the person who walks in, and praise him again. This helps to make him aware that he has to bark when someone is approaching your home. Through this training you will have a dog you can trust to guard your property. When he has

As a dog reaches maturity, he may challenge you as the dominant member of his pack.

learned to "Speak" on command, you have to train him when to stop barking. You can use words such as, "Shush", "Quiet" or "Enough"; it really will not matter. This can be achieved in the same way you taught him to "Speak". When he stops barking, say your chosen word, in a different tone of voice, and praise him.

DOMINANCE

We tend to associate dominance in a dog with one of the larger breeds. I am sorry to disillusion you, but this can be a problem with even the tiniest Yorkshire Terrier. Dominance can appear in almost any breed of dog, and there are many ways in which you may have contributed unknowingly towards your dog becoming dominant.

You, not your dog, have to be the pack leader, and he has to know that you are his senior in any situation. If you allow your dog the luxury of sleeping in your bedroom, then he definitely will assume he is leader of the pack, because he has edged his way in and conquered your territory. You should allocate just a couple of rooms in the house to him, with access only through the back door, and continue in this way until he understands that you are the person in charge, not him.

The top dog always eats first, and has the best food. Never feed him before you have eaten, and while you are eating do not allow him to stay in the same room if he pesters for tidbits. Put him in a

separate room and close the door. Continue with this approach until you feel he has understood that he will not be fed until after your meal, when it is convenient for you, and not when he demands it. Later, you can allow him into the dining-room and try again. If anyone tries to sneak tidbits to him, point out that they are not helping towards his training

Does he walk through the door before you, pushing you aside? This is a simple exercise; call him back, then walk through the door keeping him behind you until you are through the doorway.

Attention seeking from your dog has to be carefully thought about. If you know your dog is asking to be petted or played with occasionally, that is fine. However, if he regularly pushes the paper from your hands while you are reading, ask yourself if he needs re-training, or are you not spending enough play-time with him?

When my own dog reached the age of three, he decided he would not tolerate my youngest daughter, who was sixteen at the time. Whenever she walked into the room and spoke to one of us he would growl and walk away to his bed. It took time to work out what was wrong, but eventually we came to the conclusion I was the problem. I had fed him, played with him, and took him for walks, and I should have let my daughter help. To solve the problem, I first had to withdraw my attention. When he came for a cuddle I would give him one stroke and say "Good boy", then ignore him. I did not ignore him totally but if he pushed my hand I would quietly say "No, good boy, lie down". My daughter fed him (with me standing by for the first couple of days), she changed his water, and gave out his treats. This process went on for many weeks until the dog gradually relaxed with her.

AGGRESSION

Aggression by your dog must never be tolerated. If he growls when you go near his food bowl, or when he is chewing on a toy, it is time to take action. When your puppy is tiny you may laugh at the situation, but such growling outbursts will certainly not merit laughter when they come from an adult dog.

When they are small, dogs play through the use of their paws and their mouth. When your puppy comes and tries to bite at your shoe or trouser leg, place your hand over the bridge of his nose and use thumb and forefinger to curl the top lips under his upper teeth. If he tries to bite he will hurt himself and not you. Simple but effective!

A dog who is aggressive because he is nervous can be trained if he is handled with care from the

Aggression may well be the result of fear, so make sure your Airedale puppy is not frightened by a bigger dog.

A well-behaved dog is a pleasure to own.

beginning. As a puppy, he must be given as many different socialisation experiences as possible, and you must ensure that he is introduced to visitors carefully so that he regards people as friends.

It can be disastrous if your young dog is attacked by an aggressive older dog, so take care when one approaches your puppy and make sure the other dog is reliable. This happened to our friend's young Airedale, and, although the confrontation was over in minutes, the puppy never forgot, and from that day the owner had to restrain him whenever another dog so much as looked at him. His attitude was: "Let me get him before he gets me!" If your dog tries to attack other dogs you pass, talk quietly to him as the other animal passes

and keep his attention on you, perhaps offering him a tidbit. Try to use a slack lead, while keeping ample distance in case he tries to lunge at the dog. A short lead creates tension and could be misconstrued by your dog, who may think you feel threatened.

Aggression can be shown in many ways, and I have only touched the tip of the iceberg. Socialising your puppy by attending clubs and training classes may help, or your vet may be able to recommend a local trainer who appreciates and understand terriers. The Kennel Club will give you details of training classes in your area, so visit one or two, watch the classes and have a talk to the trainer to see if he can help with your special needs.

NEW CHALLENGES

With a good, basic education, your Airedale should be a well-behaved member of the family that you can take anywhere without fear of embarrassment.

You may now wish to take his training a stage further. Competitive Obedience is an exacting discipline, but the intelligent Airedale is perfectly capable of making his mark. If you are interested in getting involved, find a training club that specialises in this area.

Agility is great fun for the energetic dog and owner. The Airedale is surprisingly agile, and there is no reason why you should not have a go. Remember, your Airedale must be fully grown (over 12 months of age) before you start training. There is a large number of clubs that specialise in Agility, and they are always happy to recruit new members.

Flyball is becoming increasingly popular as a canine sport. It demands speed and a strong retrieve instinct. The dog must also learn to be single-minded and ignore he distraction of running alongside other competitors.

The versatile Aircdale can also be trained to compete in Working Trials which demand tracking as well as obedience and agility skills, and there are some Airedales who have even been trained to work as gundogs!

This is a breed that needs mental stimulation, and the more you ask of your dog, the more he will give you in return.

The intelligent Airedale can be trained to be successful in Competitive Obedience.

Agility is fun for both dog and handler.

4 The Adult Dog

By about the age of 18 months your Airedale should be eating a diet which will provide him with all he needs for a long and healthy life. There are so many feeds on the market that you should be able to find one that suits your dog. Some animals do not adapt easily to a change of diet, so, if you decide to give a different food, do so gradually, over a period of four or five days. Begin by giving three quarters of his normal feed to a quarter of the new food, increasing the quantity of the new food, and reducing his usual food accordingly.

A family pet does not need as much protein in his diet as a working dog, but, if you are uncertain about how much to give your Airedale, look at the suggested feeding requirements on the can or bag, and check his weight by the 'hands-on' method every week. I like to feed my adult dogs twice a day.

WEIGHT

The Airedale is not prone to weight problems as he is an active dog and loves to run free and play in the garden or the open fields, but some owners do overfeed. The average weight of a fully-grown Airedale varies considerably as some are very large-boned and tall, so follow the simple rule; touch and feel his body. He should have enough fat over the ribs so they do not stick out, but you should be able to feel them without difficulty. All that hair can deceive even a vet's experienced eye, so you cannot tell just by looking at him. The average weight for a bitch is around 40-50 lbs (18-23 kg) and for a dog the weight can vary from 55lbs to as much as 70lbs (25-32 kg). Size and bone play an important role; if the dog measures 24-28 inches to the shoulder he will be at the top of the weight scale, but if his height is around 23-24 inches he may only weigh around 55-60lbs. The average weight for a bitch measuring 22 inches to the shoulder is around 43-45lbs. Food for thought – please remember a dog lives much longer if he is not obese!

TOUCH

Many problems can be solved by the touch of your hands on your dog. You can use touch to check his weight, as described above, or if he seems unwell, feel him gently all over his body, legs, feet, head, ears, and mouth, and he will soon tell you where it hurts. If he gives a little whimper or growl if you touch a certain part of him, you will know you have located a sensitive area. If your dog appears to be in pain, consult the vet without delay.

KEEPING FIT

Exercise is good for you and your dog. Do not let him become bored by keeping him in the garden all the time. Get out and about, and get fit with your dog by taking him to a large field where he can roll, and run and play with you. The happiness you see in your Airedale when he is in full run, or when he bunny-hops in circles with his rear end nearly

A lean, active dog will live a longer, healthier life.

touching the floor, is something you never forget.

TEETH AND GUMS

Dogs need to have their teeth brushed every so often with a canine toothpaste to help stop tartar build-up, decay and bad breath. If tartar builds up severely, the teeth need to be scraped clean. You can do this yourself if your dog is accustomed to having his mouth checked, or your vet will be able to do this for you. A good bone to chew on also helps to keep teeth clean. Gums should be checked regularly for healthy colour, and to ensure that no

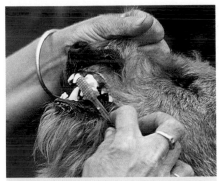
Teeth should be brushed regularly to prevent the build-up of tartar.

foreign bodies are lodged between the teeth or in the gums.

NAILS

Your dog's nails need to be kept short and neat or he will be very uncomfortable when walking. If long nails become a problem, you will have to visit the grooming parlour or your vet on a regular basis to have them cut. More

Nails will need to be trimmed if they become too long.

roadwork will help to keep them short.

EYES

The eye tells all. If your dog is unwell, his eyes will be dull to look at. If they are sore, look closely to see that no eyelashes are growing on the rim of the eyelid as this causes a little discomfort, and some Airedales do suffer this problem.

In windy weather check that no dust has got into the eye, as this can sometimes cause a slight discharge.

Bright eyes are a clear indicator that a dog is in good health.

EARS

Ears need to be kept clean, and free from hairs in the canal. This will be part of the normal routine at the grooming parlour, but you can do it yourself on a monthly basis by using your thumb and forefinger to reach into the ear canal to pull a few hairs out.

GROOMING PARLOURS

A grooming parlour has qualified staff who will bath and trim your dog as you want him to look. They have a gentle but firm approach to animals, but it is up to you to get him used to standing on the table and being brushed. If you get him used to this at home, you will find he will enjoy his visits, and it is wise to have him brushed and tangle-free before his first visit so that he will not have to be there too long. If you find the parlour makes a good job of your pet and he comes out happy, make a regular appointment for every eight or ten weeks.

If you find you enjoy trimming your dog and you want to try your hand at showing, seek the help of people who exhibit their Airedales. You can also join a breed club. Many hold lessons in grooming to help you prepare your dog for the show ring.

SHEARING

At the grooming parlour, the pet Airedale can be either hand-stripped (but this costs more) or sheared. Shearing is an easy process and less tiring for the dog than hand-stripping (see Chapter Five). A sheared dog can look very good, still keeping the black jacket (my old boy is sheared, and has a lovely black jacket), but some jackets can become very light grey after shearing. If you only want your dog to be comfortable and clean, this type of grooming is more suitable. It is also better for the older dog, as less time is spent on the table.

THE VETERAN

Old age is not a disease, but a process of progressive reduction in the efficiency and number of cells in the body. Some diseases become more common as a dog ages and, if detected early enough, can be treated before they become a real problem, so if your older dog is drinking a lot of water, or is incontinent in the night, do consult your vet for advice. The best time to give your dog a health check is when you are grooming him, as it will give you the chance to feel for any lumps under the skin. Your veteran dog

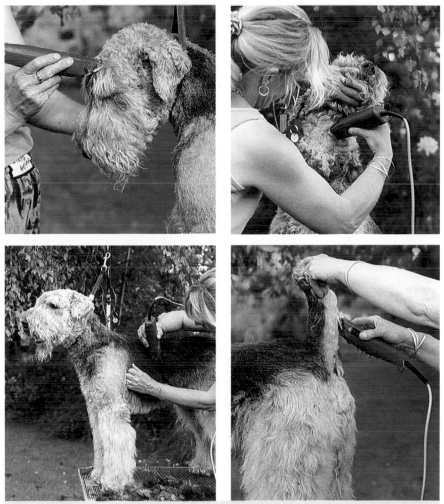

Some owners prefer to have their Airedales sheared.

should have a check-up about once a year, so that the vet can monitor his routine and give you the very best advice on caring for your old friend.

A 12-14 year old dog should be fed three times a day, and exercise controlled so that he does not get overtired. On a good day, a short car ride and a slow amble at his own pace around the woods and fields is a good idea. Always lift an old dog in and out of the car with care. His bed should be raised a little from the floor, in a warm, draught-free area, and well padded for extra comfort. Try to keep your older dog well groomed for his own comfort, just enough for his coat to be free from tangles and knots, and keep his claws short, remembering to clip the hair from inside the pads.

If the quality of life is failing in your ageing dog and your vet suggests euthanasia, it is because he knows that the time has come for you, as caring owners, to make the kindest decision. This can be the most distressing decision you will have to make, but you owe it to your dear friend to let him go without pain or suffering. The vet will do this in the familiar surroundings of your own home if you wish, and I sincerely feel it should be done this way.

The veteran Airedale should be allowed to take life at his own pace.

5

In The Show Ring

Showing can be a great hobby, but has to be given careful thought. Travelling to shows requires an early start, and the cost of travel and entry fees can be expensive, making it a costly adventure. Most exhibitors who attend the big shows are dedicated to dogs and thoroughly enjoy the day out, meeting friends from all corners of the globe. This could be you in time!

THE BREED STANDARD

All pedigree dogs are judged against the Breed Standard, a blueprint of the ideal specimen. The judge must assess all entries against this Standard, and the order of merit is decided on how

Eng & Ital Ch. Robroyd Jet: Top Airedale in Italy 1996 and 1997. Showing is an absorbing hobby, but you must be confident of having a top-quality dog.

closely each dog conforms to the Standard. Of course, the Breed Standard is open to individual interpretation, and that is why the same dog does not win at every show he is entered.

In essence the Breed Standard asks for the following points in the Airedale:

GENERAL APPEARANCE
The Airedale is the largest of the Terriers, and should be a muscular, active, and fairly cobby dog, without any suspicion of legginess or undue length of body.

CHARACTERISTICS
A quick-moving, alert dog, his temperament should show in the expression of the eyes, and by the carriage of his ears and erect tail. He should be outgoing and confident, friendly, courageous and intelligent, but not aggressive.

HEAD
The skull should be long and flat, not too broad between ears, and narrowing slightly towards the eyes. The head is well balanced, with no apparent difference in length between skull and foreface,

and without a visible stop. He should have no wrinkles, with cheeks level and free from fullness. He should not be dishfaced, nor should there be a sudden falling away below the eyes, but a delicate chiselling should prevent the appearance of wedginess or plainness. The upper and lower jaws are deep, powerful, strong and muscular, with no excess development of the jaws to give a rounded or bulging appearance to the cheeks.

The head is balanced, and the expression is keen and intelligent

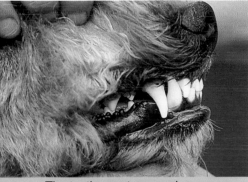

The teeth are strong and meet in a scissor bite.

The teeth and jaw should be strong, with a scissor bite. A vice-like bite is acceptable, although an overshot, or undershot, mouth is not. The lips should be tight, and the nose black.

Dark eyes, full of terrier expression, keenness and intelligence, should be small, and not prominent. Light-coloured or bold eyes are not desirable.

The ears should be V-shaped, and in proportion to the size of the dog. The top line of the folded ear must be slightly above the level of skull. Pendulous ears, or those set too high, are not acceptable.

BODY

The neck should be clean, muscular, of moderate length and thickness, gradually widening towards the shoulders, and free from throatiness. The shoulders are long, well laid back, sloping obliquely, with the shoulder blades flat. The forelegs must be perfectly straight with good bone, and the elbows perpendicular to the body, working free of the sides.

The back is short, strong, straight and level, showing no slackness, the loins muscular, and the ribs well sprung. In short-coupled and well ribbed-up dogs there is little space between ribs and hips. The chest should be deep, approximately level with elbows, but not broad.

The thighs are long and powerful with a muscular second

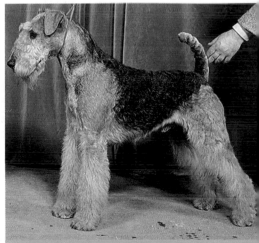

A muscular, active dog with a short, strong back, and a deep chest.

thigh, the stifles well bent, and turned neither in nor out. The hocks are well let down, and parallel when viewed from behind. The feet are small, round, and compact, well cushioned, with good depth of pad, and the toes moderately arched, turning neither in nor out.

The tail, which is customarily docked, should be set on high and carried gaily, with good strength and substance, and not curled over the back. The tip of the tail should be level with the top of the skull.

GAIT
When in motion, the legs are carried straight forward, with the forelegs moving freely, and parallel to the sides. From the front, the forelegs should form a continuation of the straight line in front, with the feet the same distance apart as the elbows. Propulsive power is provided by the hind legs.

COAT
The Airedale coat should be hard, dense, wiry, and not so long as to appear ragged. It should lay straight and close, covering body and legs, with the outer coat hard, wiry and stiff, and the undercoat shorter and softer. The hardest

coats crinkle or are just slightly waved; curly or soft coats are not acceptable. The body saddle, top of the neck, and of the tail, should be black or grizzle, with all other parts tan. The ears are often a darker tan, and shading may occur round the neck and sides of the skull. A few white hairs between the forelegs is acceptable.

SIZE
The height standard is about 58-61 cms (23-24 ins) to the top of the shoulder for dogs, and about 56-59 cms (22-23 ins) for bitches.

PRESENTATION
The Airedale must look his best in order to do himself justice, and this also involves a lot of hard work. Hand-stripping is a skilled task that requires many hours work to achieve the finish that you see in the show ring. The breeder may let you watch him or her prepare a dog for show, or you could use a grooming parlour that can make your Airedale look nearly as good as a show dog. For the brave, a picture or photograph of a good Airedale pinned on the wall will help.

You should begin with your puppy from the age of 10-12 weeks, just working enough to keep the coat flat and removing any straggly hair from the legs. Do not keep your puppy on the grooming-table for long periods, and when you have finished, play with him and offer a tidbit to make it seem fun. When he is around five to six months and can stand without a second person helping to hold him safe, it is time to begin the process of helping to make him look like the King of Terriers.

Hand-stripping: A step-by-step guide
Words and photos: Steph Holbrook.

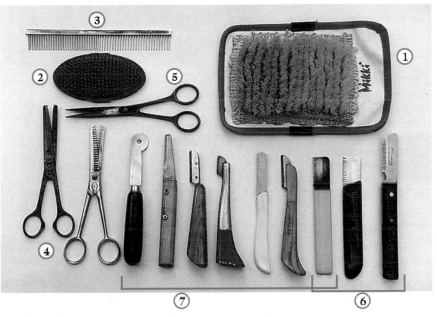

(1) *Basic grooming equipment illustrated with an assortment of knives. To begin with, find a knife that is comfortable to use and practise as much as possible.*
1. Bristle glove (for polishing)
2. Pin-pad
3. Comb
4. Fine and coarse thinning scissors
5. Straight scissors
6. A selection of knives (also suitable for raking)
7. Medium and fine knives.

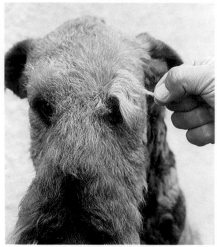

② *Before stripping, but brushed out to look his best. This dog has eight weeks of coat growth since his last strip, and the untidy coat does nothing to enhance his conformation. He appears coarse in head, thick in neck and a little heavy in the forehand. Rough leg hair spoils his movement and his feet look large.*

④ *Properly finished eyebrows will help that typical 'terrier' expression. Looking from the front of the head, comb the eyebrows to the side. Carefully finger-pluck to remove hairs that stray beyond the straight line of the side cheek and muzzle. The eyebrows should not be over-long.*

③ *(Right) The head and expression is a vitally important part of presentation; it can complete or spoil an otherwise good trim, so attention to fine detail is essential.*

To strip the coat, grip the tips of just a few hairs between your thumb and the knife blade, and pluck out sharply. Always tug the hair in the direction it grows. It helps if you keep the skin taut with your other hand, and this also makes it more comfortable for the dog. In some areas, such as the foreface, it is better to use finger and thumb rather than a knife.

Leave the foreface hair until later, and strip the skull and cheeks very close.

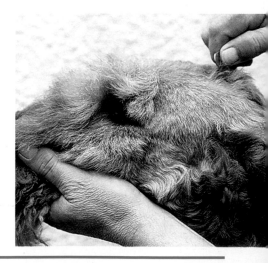

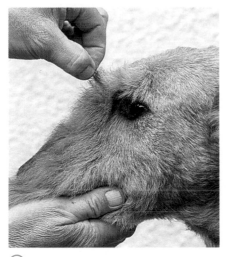

(5) Comb the eyebrows forward and thin the hair at the outside corner of the eye.

(6) Reduce the fullness of the coat just above the inside corner of the eye so the eyebrows will sit smoothly, flush with the foreface. Finish the muzzle and whiskers later.

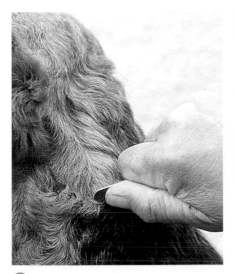

(8) Continue to close strip down the length of the side neck, on to the shoulder and upper arm, almost to the front leg. Blend the shorter hair into the top of the leg hair.

Now strip the remaining hair from close to the corners of the mouth, under the jaws and throat, down the front neck and chest to the front legs. Leave some fringe to sit between the front legs at the bottom of the chest.

(7) Leaving the longer hair at the centre back of the skull and neck, continue to strip very close to the sides of the neck.

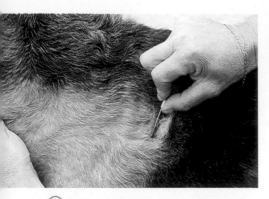

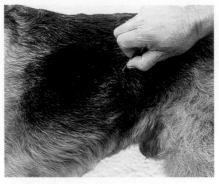

⑨ Rake to remove some undercoat before blending the shorter hair on the shoulder into the medium length body hair.

The amount of raking needed on the ribs, back loin and upper thighs will vary. The Airedale should have both topcoat and undercoat in these areas.

⑩ Once established, a regular stripping routine will rotate the coat. Here, pale, dead hair is being stripped from the ribs and loin, leaving fresh, darker, shorter hair. By the time this new hair needs stripping, another layer will be well on its way.

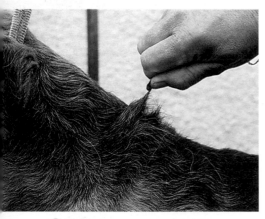

⑪ The topline, which goes from the skull, down the ridge of the neck, over the withers and back to the base of the tail, should be as even as possible, uninterrupted by dips or bumps.

⑫ The tail should be stripped to medium thickness – not too close. The back of the tail should be stripped fairly short, and thinning scissors can be used for this. The tip of the tail should be rounded using thinning scissors.

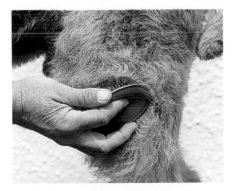

⑬ To prevent hair from breaking, spray the legs with water before using the pin-pad with a gentle, massaging, rotating action.

⑭ Make sure the dog is standing in a comfortable, balanced position, lift and tidy each foot by scissoring away excess hair. Take care not to over-trim between the pads. The dog needs some hair for protection.

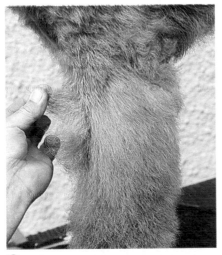

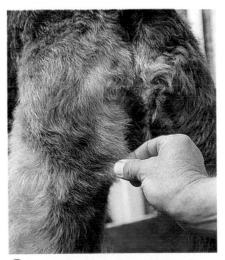

⑮ After using the pid-pad on the forelegs, gently comb the hair down into place. Then selectively remove long hairs to straighten and neaten the overall shape. Check the dog's movement in case you need to make adjustments.

⑯ The rear of the upper inner thigh should be stripped short. This is one of the more sensitive areas, so take care and be patient. Lightly strip the back of the leg to show the turn of stifle.

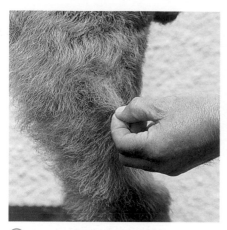

17 The hip and side thigh hair, which is short to medium, should blend into the longer hair of the front thigh and stifle. After combing the hair into place, remove only the longer hairs that interfere with the clean outline of the dog.

18 After tidying the feet as much as possible with a stripping knife, plus finger and thumb stripping, finish the lower edges with scissors to make the feet look small, round and compact. Note the finished shape of the hock.

19 The hindquarter on the left is finished. The right-hand side still shows eight weeks of growth.

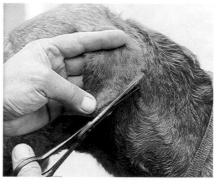

20 The ears are very sensitive, so use a fine stripping knife. Work very slowly, stripping just a few hairs at a time. A nicked ear bleeds profusely and takes weeks to heal.
Completely clear the underside of the ears by stripping, scissoring, or a combination of both. A couple of days before a show, scissor the ears close.

(21)*(Right) Softly, softly here, taking a very few hairs at a time, blend the foreface gently into the cheeks. Checking frequently, shape the muzzle and whiskers to sit flat at the sides and top of the face. Do not over-trim. The muzzle should not appear weak or snipey.*

(22)*The finished result. Conformation is now enhanced and the dog is showing himself to advantage. After this strip, his coat will need attention at least every two days over several weeks to ensure a good, hard, tight jacket.*

SHOW TRAINING

It is not enough for you to turn up at a show with your Airedale and hope for the best. Many hours of hard work go into training the dog to show himself off to advantage. Show dogs must learn to stand in the correct pose, and to move at the correct gait.

There are two methods of posing the Airedale – free standing, where the dog stands naturally on a loose lead, or stacked where the dog is placed in position.

The method you choose is a matter of personal preference, but if you choose the free standing method you have to be confident that your Airedale has excellent tail-set.

Many breed and training clubs hold monthly or weekly sessions to help the expert and novice, be it dog or handler, to improve their ringcraft.

It is also a place where you can get feedback from people who have entered a dog or dogs at a recent show and learn different techniques used in the show ring.

Social interaction of this kind gives the handler, and dog, a confident and happy approach to showing.

1. The collar placement is checked to ensure it is in the correct position on the neck.

2. The front leg (nearest the judge) is placed.

3. The other front leg is put into position.

5. The hindquarters are put into the correct position.

4. Run your hand down the back to place the hindquarters.

6. The correct show pose.

7. The judge will assess movement from the front...

8. ...in profile...

9. ...and from the rear.

EXHIBITING

You will need to take with you to the show a dog crate (optional), grooming-table, grooming-box, a small first-aid box, water and bowl, a towel, and lunch!

When entering your first show, send off for the schedule in advance. If you find the entry form daunting, seek the help of your breeder or someone who shows regularly to help you fill in the details. Do choose the correct class – you do not enter a puppy in the Open class, for example – and resist the impulse to enter too many classes when first exhibiting; one or two classes is enough for any novice. The closing date for entries will be on the form so return it, with the entry fee, in good time.

The few days of preparation before the show can be hectic, so keep a calendar in your grooming area or anywhere you can make notes of your plan of action. You should have been working on the grooming of your dog for some months, and his legs, underbody and facial beard can be bathed a couple of days before the show, making the finishing touches to his feet and ears at the same time. Do not make the mistake of having to strip your dog at the

Free standing: This style of handling requires considerable skill.

Stacked: The handler is presenting the dog to full advantage.

show, as he will not want to be pulled about at that time, especially after a journey. It should be a happy time for both dog and owner. All that is required at the show for the final preparation is to brush up and to comb the hair into place just before he goes into the ring.

If you do not know what time you are supposed to be in the ring, do not panic. Just ask one of the other exhibitors what time judging is to commence. Try to work out how much time you will need to prepare your dog for the ring, so that your young puppy is not on the table for too long.

When you enter the ring, the steward will ask you to stand in line with the other exhibitors (much as you practised in training classes).

The judge will call the exhibitors in turn and assess each one against the Breed Standard, before explaining how he would like you to walk your dog. When he has assessed all the dogs, keep an eye on the judge as he looks at the line.

Remember, win or lose, showing is meant to be enjoyable for both dog and handler. Enjoy the good days, and always be sporting to other exhibitors.

6 Breeding Airedales

Any breeding programme has to be thought out very carefully, because rearing a litter is costly, hard work, and takes up many hours of your time. A bitch is not better for having a litter, so do not fall into the trap of mating her for this reason.

If you are sure you want to breed from her, your bitch has to be mature and healthy. She must be sound in both mind and body.

Many Airedales do not have their first season until they are nine to twelve months of age and some are as late as eighteen months.

At about this time, have her checked by the vet to make sure she has no hereditary faults and is of good type, and take the opportunity to have her hip-scored, as this must be done well in advance of mating.

It is usual to mate an Airedale for the first time after she has had her third season, sometimes later.

THE STUD DOG

You should choose the stud dog with care, making sure he is sound and typical of the breed in type and temperament, and as near the Breed Standard as possible. He does not need to be a Champion, but if you see or hear of a dog that has sired good puppies with all the characteristics of an Airedale, and he complements your bitch, the choice is easy. You can also ask the breeder of your bitch for advice.

You may have to travel some distance to the dog of your choice, but this is a normal procedure. His owner will need to know the first day of your bitch's season, so that he can make the necessary arrangements for your visit. A bitch can be ready to mate at the onset of her season, or as late as her thirtieth day, but generally between the ninth and the twentieth day. Mating is usually straightforward and the stud dog

The stud dog you choose must be sound in mind and body, and he must be a typical specimen of the breed.

owner will usually ask you to bring her again two days later for a second mating, so you may care to leave the bitch at the stud dog's home, if they have the facilities.

Your bitch must be kept away from other dogs until her cycle has ended, as she may still want to mate and this could cause problems.

THE PREGNANT BITCH

Pregnancy lasts for an average of 63 days (nine weeks), but it is not unusual for the bitch to deliver a couple of days either side of the due date. Your bitch should be allowed to carry on with her usual routine; she is not sick, so feeding and exercise should remain as normal. A thorough grooming in the early stages is a good idea as she may become uncomfortable later. You should notice signs of pregnancy around six or seven weeks after mating, with increased body weight, and swelling of the abdomen, but, if the bitch is carrying only a few pups, there may be little or no sign. When she is lying quietly outstretched, you may be able to see slight movement in the abdomen, and this is the time to increase her normal food by 30-60 per cent, with a higher protein level. Do not increase her food until this stage as it will only lead to your Airedale becoming vastly overweight.

A viscid discharge in the pregnant bitch is noticed from approximately thirty-two days, and, if this is not apparent, she is usually not pregnant. Your vet will advise on worming procedures. A thorough worming programme will not prevent the bitch passing worms to her pups, but the best time to worm is well before mating, and again when the suckling pups are old enough.

When you are certain she is pregnant, the preparation of you bitch's quarters must begin, as you will want her to be relaxed and familiar in the surroundings where she is to whelp. Do not leave this to the last moment, or you may find she wants to deliver on your bed! Choose a quiet room away from the main doors into your home, as she will not want visitors peeping in when she is due to deliver, or when feeding her puppies in the early stages. The room must be draught-free, and a temperature maintained around 25 degrees C for the first four weeks. A heat pad or overhead heat-lamp is useful, and this should be checked by placing a thermometer on the floor of the box directly under the lamp. The whelping box should be of ample size for the bitch to lie outstretched, with room to spare at each end. One side should have easy access for the bitch to walk in and out but be high enough to stop the puppies falling out. Place plenty of newspaper under the bedding for insulation. Try to get your bitch used to eating and sleeping in the room for a minimum of two weeks before whelping.

WHELPING

About twenty-four hours before whelping, some bitches may refuse food, and this is often thought to be an infallible prediction of the onset of parturition. However, most of my bitches eat well right up to, and during, birth, so I do not find this method very reliable. Your bitch will scratch at the newspaper and tear her bedding to prepare a nest, and may show some unease, interspersed with

Do not change diet or routine until the bitch is 6-7 weeks into her pregnancy.

periods of rest. This first stage can last for as long as forty-eight hours, so a baby intercom, or a video camera, are useful to monitor your bitch without disturbing her too often

During this first stage, when the bitch is panting, the cervix is dilating and the pups are changing position ready for their journey into the world. The vulva is puffy, large and very moist and begins to excrete a white or creamy discharge.

It is important to record the time when the main contractions begin, as the vet will need to know this if complications occur.

There are intervals of rest during contractions, but, if your bitch is pushing hard for longer than two hours, veterinary help should be sought immediately. Generally the pup comes out still inside the inner membrane and the bitch may break the sac herself, but a maiden bitch may need your help. Tear the sac with your fingers, trying to keep the head of the puppy upwards, to allow the mucus to flow away from the head. Wipe the pup's face with a piece of kitchen roll so that he cannot suck in fluid with his first breath. The placenta almost always comes immediately afterwards, and the bitch bites the umbilical cord, before eating the placenta. If she needs help, hold the cord firmly with the finger and thumb of one hand and tear the cord with the other, taking care not to pull at the pup's stomach. The placenta contains nutrients for the bitch, but in extra-large litters it is best not to let her eat them all. Write down the time of birth and note if the placenta was there. It is quite natural for the bitch to roll the pup over and lick him to dry the mucus and help him breathe. The pup will usually want to suckle immediately if the birth did not take too long, but sometimes you can help by holding a teat and gently working the fingers to release the milk while holding the puppy to it. He will usually attach himself like a leech to the teat and suckle heartily. The interval between puppies can be as long as four hours, or as short as twenty minutes. Some bitches stop whelping after six or seven puppies, and can still produce one or more the next day! Enjoy the moment to just sit and watch the wonders of nature, but on no account allow visitors to take a peek at this stage.

Keep a bowl of fresh water with a little milk or glucose added, to offer your bitch if she wants it. She may also, after the long hours of whelping, need to go out to relieve herself. Offer her a light meal of chicken, or scrambled eggs with cheese (a favourite), cheese flan, or fish, but bear in mind that, having eaten the afterbirths, she may not want to eat for a while. Her motions will naturally be a little loose for the first few days.

When the bitch is settled and finished, arrange for the vet to make a home visit when convenient, to give both the mother and pups a check-up.

POST WHELPING

There is very little to do over the next three weeks, as the puppies will be cared for by their mother. The bitch's discharge will be fairly heavy for the first few days, as the process of cleansing the uterus can take as long as three to four weeks, changing in colour from brown to red and becoming lighter.

Continue to feed your bitch a light diet, little and often, for a few days, but ensure she has a good high-protein food to provide plenty of calcium. If the level of calcium falls, she could suffer a condition known as eclampsia, causing her to ignore her pups,

look starry-eyed, shake, whine or pant uncontrollably. If she shows any of these symptoms seek veterinary advice immediately as she could go into a coma and die.

Feel around the nipples regularly to check that she is not suffering from mastitis. This can be relieved by holding a warm poultice against the hardened teat and gently squeezing out some of the milk. Put one of the greedy pups onto that teat for the next few

Most Airedales adapt well to motherhood and are very tolerant of their puppies.

Time is divided between eating, sleeping and playing.

days and it should soon clear up.

At three to four days, the dew-claws need to be cut, and the tails docked by a vet. The Breed Standard says 'customarily docked'. Docking has to be arranged well in advance of the litter being born, as the owner needs to be a member of The Council of Docked Breeds in order to gain access to a list of vets who are prepared to carry out this procedure. Docking is illegal in the UK unless it is carried out by a vet.

Keep the puppies' nails short by trimming with scissors or they will scratch their dam's tummy as they suckle and she will become very sore

At ten to fifteen days the puppies' eyes begin to open, and they become more active in the box.

69

TWO TO EIGHT WEEKS

A worming programme can be planned, with the help of your vet, giving accurate doses according to the weight of the puppies.

This may be the time to move the puppies and mum into outside quarters, if you have not already done so, as they need more space at this stage.

Your bitch will want to spend a little time away from the pups, but not be out of earshot. A sleeping area, placed high enough for her to lie comfortably without being pestered, will help.

The puppies will start to climb out of the box to play, and relieve themselves. All those old newspapers you have been saving will come into their own now as they can be used on the floor of the puppy area and, when soiled, can be easily rolled up and disposed of.

Begin weaning by encouraging the pups to lap a milky porridge specially developed for them. This is a messy time for everyone, but such fun to watch. Other foods can gradually be introduced, and the complete foods do make life easier at this stage. Make sure that there is clean water available at all times. Feed every three hours at first, gradually decreasing to four-hourly intervals, but always making the last feed of the day about an hour before you go to bed.

SOCIALISING PUPPIES

Puppies must receive plenty of attention and get used to being handled if they are to become well-adjusted pets. If they bite at you, growl at them, just as their mother does when they misbehave. Provide toys for them to chew, and give them plenty of free play in the garden with mum, where they can explore, exercise and become fit. When you call to their mother, they will usually follow, learning to respond to the human voice. Clatter their bowls at feeding time, and leave a radio on so that they get used to different sounds and surroundings. This will help make bold, well-adjusted puppies ready to go to their new owners.

Do vet prospective buyers very carefully, and pry a little into their background. You want your puppies to go to caring homes. The usual age to let the puppy go to his new owners is eight weeks, and do have everything prepared when they arrive to collect him. You will need the pedigree and the registration, ready to sign at the time of sale, a guide to his feeding routine, and a note of when worming is due again. When the puppy leaves for his new home your legal responsibility ends, but the majority of breeders keep in contact to offer advice and, if by chance the new owners have some crisis and the dog needs to be re-homed, a good breeder will take the puppy or dog back and find him a new home.

At eight weeks of age, the puppies will be ready to leave for their new homes.

7 *Health Matters*

Airedales are generally healthy animals, but naturally some do have health problems from time to time. You will soon notice if your dog is unwell; if he is lethargic, off his food, or even eating abnormally large amounts.

The main warning signs to watch for are the drinking of abnormal amounts of water, vomiting, diarrhoea, breathing difficulties or coughing, bleeding in any area, scratching, discharging, sore, swollen, or light-sensitive eyes, head shaking, swollen or discharging ears, limping, blood in the urine or urinating too often, and pain when passing a motion.

Consult the vet immediately if your dog shows any of the following symptoms: collapse, vomiting and/or diarrhoea for more than twenty-four hours, cramp, trouble breathing, bleeding, signs of pain or discomfort, drinking abnormal amounts, or heatstroke. Any cause for concern, especially in puppies or older dogs, should be referred to your vet, and help him by giving him an accurate history of your dog's condition. It is a good idea to write it down, because, if you are anxious about your pet, you can easily forget to mention a vital piece of information.

INTERNAL PARASITES
Regular worming of an adult dog should be done every six months if in contact with children, but once a year can be sufficient for many dogs. Worms can cause a dull coat, swelling of the stomach, loss of weight, pneumonia, and diarrhoea. In addition, one of the commonest roundworms, Toxocara canis, is easily transmitted to children, and can cause potentially permanent eye damage. A multi-wormer supplied by your vet will rid the dog of all types of worms. You must weigh

your dog accurately before administering this type of drug as overdose is possible, so be sure toread the label and give the exact amount advised for the weight of your dog. Many wormers on the market are much too strong for young, sensitive stomachs, and should not be given while your puppy is in the middle of his course of vaccinations. However effective the wormer recommended by your vet, re-infestation can occur so a few simple precautions should be taken:

• Effective flea control for your dog, and your home, helps reduce the transmission of the flea tapeworm.

• Avoid feeding raw offal or unsterilised foods.

• Train your dog to use a certain area in your garden for his toilet and keep children away from that area. Clean up faeces straight away (always carry a strong plastic bag or poop scoop).

EXTERNAL PARASITES

Dog fleas are different from those which infest humans and cats. When a flea bites, it injects saliva to stop the blood clotting whilE it is sucked up. This saliva contains chemicals which can create an

allergic reaction, causing large areas of inflammation on the dog's back. If your dog is scratching, or you find black gritty material in the coat, or bites which look like small red pimples, get a spray from your vet and read the instructions very carefully. When using a spray, try to do so outside with the wind blowing away from both you and your pet, so that

neither of you inhale it. A household spray should also be bought to treat your pet's bed area, and your home, throughout the summer months.

Tried and tested remedies
Mix six drops of lavender oil, two drops of tea-tree oil and two tablespoonfuls of water in a spray container, and treat your dog's coat, bedding and carpets with it. The smell is lovely, but fleas hate it!

You can also give your dog garlic tablets and brewers yeast, or garlic and fenugreek tablets, or bathe him in Oil of Olay soap to deter fleas from settling on him.

LICE AND TICKS

There are two types of lice that affect dogs; ones which feed on flakes of skin, and sucking lice. The latter cause skin irritation as they penetrate the skin to feed on tissue fluids (neither will spread to humans or cats). Lice are grey and lay small eggs which stick to the dog's hair. Treat your dog with sprays or baths, three or four times at five to seven-day intervals, to kill the adults and any hatching larvae.

The sheep tick is the most common type found on dogs. It attaches itself with its mouth part through the skin, and, as it sucks the dog's blood, its abdomen swells. It is usually found on the belly, under the forelegs and on the head, and it is important that you do not try to pull it off. A flea spray should be applied locally, and the tick removed the next day, when it is dead. It can also be dabbed with alcohol (gin or methylated spirits will do) and dislodged after a few minutes. It is important to remove the head or an abscess may form. If the head does remain behind, warm compresses may help to draw out the infection, combined with antibacterial washes and creams.

Tried and tested remedies

Ticks have a screw-like structure on their heads. They bore into the tissues by turning anti-clockwise and release themselves by turning clockwise. A tick can therefore be 'unscrewed' by turning it round several times in a clockwise direction, while applying gentle traction. The head, with it dreaded pincers, will not tear off with this method, avoiding the complication of an abscess forming.

PARVOVIRUS

This is one of the most deadly viral infections in dogs. Young puppies and older dogs are more at risk. Public parks, where a lot of dogs are walked, are high-risk areas and any faeces on your shoes can carry the infection into your home. The symptoms are lethargy, vomiting, and blood-stained diarrhoea. Seek veterinary help immediately.

INFECTIOUS BRONCHITIS

This term is now used to describe bronchial infections in dogs, which is far more appropriate than the old name of 'kennel cough'. The old term implied that it was prevalent in boarding kennels, but dogs are just as likely to become

infected at dogs shows, training classes, in the park, or even at the veterinary surgery.

The cough can be harsh and dry, and begin quite suddenly, sounding as though your dog may have something stuck in his throat and is trying to vomit. The sides of the neck will be swollen and temperature may be raised.

If you suspect a cough you should take your dog to the vet without delay, but tell your vet before you take your dog into the

waiting room, and he will probably arrange for you to wait outside until he can see you, as the condition is highly infectious and you could be putting his other patients at risk.

Even after the symptoms have subsided, dogs can remain infectious for up to three months.

ITCHY SKIN

Airedales can suffer skin problems, but not as readily as some other breeds. If your pet is constantly scratching, and you have ruled out the presence of fleas, try changing his diet, and monitor him for three or four weeks. Feed a low-protein food such as chicken and rice.

Some dogs are allergic to flea sprays, and the flea repellent that is applied as drops between the shoulder blades.

Animals can be allergic to grass, but only very rarely does this occur in an Airedale.

ANAL GLANDS

There are two such glands in the dog, situated slightly below, and to each side of, the anus. If the ducts become blocked the secretions from the glands cannot escape, causing swelling. If there is an infection the normal secretion

is replaced by a brownish, foul-smelling pus, causing irritation or pain. If your dog yelps when he sits down, chases his tail, drags his rear end on the ground, or carries his tail low, check to see if there is any sign of swelling. You may be able to clear blocked ducts by placing a few sheets of kitchen roll over the anus and gentle squeezing with finger and thumb on either side of the anus. If this does not work, there are spots of blood, or your dog is in pain, seek veterinary help.

HEATSTROKE

Overheating can be dangerous for any dog, so when you take him out for walks in summer make sure it is early morning or late at night. Never shut your pet in a hot room in the summer, and never leave him in a car while you go shopping! If you do find yourself with a dog who is in distress through heat, get him to water immediately, and wet him all over to reduce his body heat, then take him immediately to the vet.

CHOCOLATE ALLERGY

Theobromine, which is found in chocolate (dark cooking-chocolate contains the most), is highly toxic to dogs. The effect is dependant on the amount eaten, and he may only suffer slight diarrhoea, but it could trigger cardiac irregularity, or epileptic fits. The best policy is to avoid giving your pet any chocolate.

HIP DYSPLASIA

The Airedale, being a large dog, can suffer from hip dysplasia, but it is not as common as in some breeds Most breeders have their breeding stock hip-scored by having the hip joints X-rayed by the vet. This helps to select good stock for breeding, and dogs that do not meet the required standard should not be bred from.

If you notice that your puppy or young dog will not walk for long periods, or has difficulty rising from a sitting or prone position, discuss the problem with your vet, who may X-ray the hips and, if necessary, suggest one of the many surgical options available.

CONGENITAL EYE PROBLEMS

Entropion is a condition where the eyelid turns inwards, causing the lashes to dig into the surface of the eye, making it red and very sore.

Ectropion causes the eyelids to turn outwards allowing tears to pool in the pouch formed by the lid and causing the cornea to dry out.

Trichiasis is the condition where a dog's eyelashes grow in the wrong direction so they rub on the eye causing pain.

Distichiasis is a similar problem, where extra hairs grow on the edge of the lid and rub the eye.

All these eye problems, if left untreated, may cause serious

damage, even blindness. Fortunately, they can all be treated, but, if your dog suffers any of the above conditions he should not be included in your breeding programme, as they can all be passed on to progeny.

PETS BEAT STRESS

The unconditional love that a pet can offer does help people to relax. Research has shown that simply stroking a dog or cat can be an instant remedy for stress, and the mere presence of a pet seems to have a calming effect on animal lovers. The relaxation we feel when stroking an animal can be measured as a reduction in heartbeat and a fall in blood pressure, so for people suffering from raised blood pressure or hypertension, the benefit of

having a pet can be equated with eating a low-salt diet or drinking less alcohol.

Studies conducted in Australia indicate that dog owners visit their doctor eight per cent less than non-owners, while cat owners had a twelve per cent lower attendance rate. These statistics are reflected in lower rates of medication used to control heart problems, sleeping difficulties, high blood pressure and cholesterol levels.

It has been found that children in hospital who suffer depression and stress brought on by long term illness and unpleasant clinical treatment, have benefited from animals being brought into the ward to help them overcome their anxieties.